The CRAZY Adventures of Steve: A Minecraft Novel

By
Minecraft Novels

Table of Contents

Chapter One – A Dream Come True

"I need your help dear brother," a distant but familiar voice rang through my mind, "you're the last hope of this world now." Everything around me seemed oddly unreal, the cube blocks were floating strangely; they seemed to somehow flow like smoke in the wind. The voice echoed back around "I have failed in my mission, the dragon still lives... They have taken me hostage and are planning a massive attack." The voice slowly trailed off.

I slowly came to the realization that the echoing voice belonged to my older brother, Preston, a soldier in the Greenskeeper army. I hadn't heard from him since he left for the war months and months ago.

All of a sudden the world seemed to get darker and a massive strike of thunder boomed overhead "We don't have much time left together", my brother's voice reverberated overhead, "you need to destroy the Chain of Power. It is how they are able to keep the Dragon under their power. If the chain is destroyed, the dragon will be freed!" The wind was picking up and the world was only getting darker.

"But how am I suppose to do all of that?!" I shouted with despair, "I've never even fought so much as a single zombie!" It was true. I was never the adventurous type. I always stayed in my little spawn area and built up all kinds of things. I never went out and fought. My older brother Preston was the one who did all of that.

"You must find a way Steve, or the world as we know it will come to an end." With every passing word my brother's voice was getting more and more faint as the wind picked up. "Go to the Great Mountain. Deep in its bowels, you will find the Ender Dragon protecting the Chain of Power." The world began to spin as everything grew much darker. The wind was speeding up to a powerful, roaring screech. "Use the amulet! The Amulet of the Dragon," I could barely hear Preston's voice over the wind, "Get into the mountains through the base of the last tree standing!"

I woke up with a shock; I was covered in sweat and could barely remember what had just happened... Did I speak with my brother? I recalled feeling extremely worried, like something terrible just happened. Was my brother captured by the Huntsmen? Was Herobrine behind this? Is that what had happened? Well, it was only a dream. It doesn't mean anything, right?

Later that day I went back to doing what I always do, building out my massive structures, my castles, my towers, and today my new maze. I was always a littler faster than everyone else at building, for I could place down ten blocks of stone in the time it took some people to lay down five.

My two best friends were helping me out today, Jack and Tom. They both spend most of their days out here building with me and staying away from the more dangerous side of the world. I wouldn't say we haven't thought about venturing out and exploring, but a chance to do so never really presented itself.

"How tall did you want the walls of this maze to be, Steve?" Tom asked. He was always the calculating one, both serious and quite cautious. Jack cut in "about as high as it needs to be I reckon." Jack on the other hand was much more laid back; he built more for fun than anything else. I called out "at least three or four blocks tall, we don't want anyone jumping out – " BOOOOM! A massive explosion from over the hill cut me off. BOOM, BOOM, BOOOOM, every last explosion shook the ground beneath us - even the maze was shuddering.

Finally, the explosions in the distance died out. We jumped down from our in-construction maze and began to sprint over to the source of the attack. We passed through our town on the way. Everyone was in full panic around us, running back and forth, trying to gather up their belongings and pack up their horses. It seemed like the explosions must have hit the village over. I could just make out a woman's screams as she ran past, "… they've never hit so far east! We have to leave, we could be next…"

I looked back at Jack and Tom; they had the same panicked look in their eyes. We knew we had to get out of here as soon as possible. Thinking on my feet, I said "Grab what you need from your houses and pack it quick. We'll meet back up at the barn."

I sprinted as fast as I could back to my house; it was on the far side of my little town. I ran right through the wheat farm - I don't think anyone will care about that now. As soon as I ran back through the door I flung open my chest and grabbed as much as I could. I grabbed iron armor, a compass, my grandfather's amulet, and the sword my brother gave to me last year. I was out of there almost as fast as I got in.

I was heading straight for the barn when I ran headlong into a group of Greenskeeper soldiers. I was knocked over by the beast of the sergeant in front. Thankfully they didn't seem to notice me. "… It had to have been creepers. Nothing else has that kind of power" one of the soldiers was saying, "Besides, those coward Huntsmen don't actually do any of the fighting themselves. Herobrine has the creepers do everything for them." As it was, the creepers were somehow being bred by the Huntsmen. More and more of them appeared every day.

"This village has little time left" the sergeant sharply cut in, "in truth we're doing much worse than it seems. We're losing this war…" Everyone quieted down. The sergeant slowly and sadly said,

"The capitol was hit early today, along with several other major cities. We're on our own now, boys..." He slowly went on "and that's not all... Lieutenant Preston's undercover mission failed. He was captured right before he had a chance to strike at the heart of the enemy, I could only just get out of there with a few other men without being either captured or blown up by creepers..."

Preston! Captured? Just like in my dream! It wasn't just a dream then! He was trying to communicate with me... What else did he say? Dang! Why can't I remember...? This dream is much more important than I could have ever imaged... Think, Steve, think! Something about a chain that I had to destroy... Yes! It was in the Great Mountain!

Which is in the middle of enemy territory… How am I ever going to get there? Let alone get into the mountain past an ender dragon and somehow destroy the chain of power?! It's hopeless… not even my brother could do it.

The soldiers quietly rode away after hearing the terrible news from their sergeant. All I could hear was the slow clop of the horses' hooves as they rode out into the distance towards the destroyed village over. I couldn't just let go of what my brother told me. I can't just give up and roll over. But I've never gone on an adventure; I've never even used my sword! But there was no one else to do it, no one else knew what I knew, and my brother had trusted me with this. He didn't trust anyone else. I have to give it my best shot. I don't know if I'll be able to do it or if I'll even make it there in one piece. But I have to try! I have to give it my best shot!

And with that I was off, running as fast as I could, sprinting the entire way to the barn. I bumped into a few people and a couple of free flying chickens as I ran. Both of my friends were already waiting there with three horses saddled up. "What took so long?" Jack asked. I quickly explained to them everything that had happened to me today and what I was planning on setting out to do. "Well, we're coming with you" Tom spoke up, "we won't let you do this alone." Jack agreed, "We can finally go on an adventure!" After a few minutes they had convinced me. Maybe I could make it a little further with their help.

We set out and rode our horses all day long and well into the night. We were heading west, into the war stricken lands. We finally decided to stop at an inn along the way; after all, we did need somewhere to rest. We went up to the innkeeper and asked for a room for the night. "That will be 10 emeralds; in times like these, everything is expensive." The innkeeper said. We paid him the emeralds. "You have the last room on the left, room 107."

"And be careful out there, they said that the great respawners were destroyed last night… anyone who dies now… won't come back."

We headed to our room in solemn silence as we processed the grave news told by the innkeeper… The respawners were the only things keeping the danger from ever truly impacting anyone. Now they were gone and no one would be able to respawn after they die. "I understand if you guys don't want to come with me anymore, but I'm still going." I muttered. "We're still with you Steve, we're going to end this war even if it's the last thing we do!" Jack said with shaky passion. We made it to our small room and climbed into the small wood framed beds. With the looming thought of what we had to do on our minds we tried to fall asleep. I clutched my grandfather's old amulet to my chest as I finally drifted into a restless sleep.

The next morning we all got up, stretching our stiff bodies and silently walked down the hall for breakfast before heading out. The Innkeeper greeted us with a serious look on her face. "Your horses have been watered and groomed, they should be okay for a few more days of travel." "Thank you," I said as we took our seats at a table in the back corner of the breakfast hall.

We ordered our breakfast and began to quietly go over our plans for the day when the innkeeper's daughter brought bread and mushroom stew. "Have you heard?" The innkeeper's daughter said. "Another town has been hit by creepers, my mother is very upset." We looked over to see the innkeeper staring sightlessly out the window. "The town which was hit was home to my mother's closest of friends. Word is that no one escaped the devastation those creepers left behind."

The innkeeper's daughter walked away from our table to deliver food to the other travelers. I watched her walk away then turned to my bread and soup and began to eat in silence. After our breakfast we walked out to the stables, which sat right next to the inn. We found our horses saddled and ready to go.

It was a chilly morning with blocks of clouds moving across the sky. "Do you both have your armor and weapons?" I asked. "Yes, but I pray we will not need them." Tom replied.

With a last look back at the small inn we steered our horses down the dirt path toward the Great Mountain and the dragon within its depths. After hours of riding we hit our first roadblock. A great crevasse ran through the road and continued on for as far as the eye could see. The gorge was hundreds of blocks deep. "Well, there's no way we can ride our horses down that" Tom remarked. "I guess we will have to walk them down, nice and slow" I replied. So, we dismounted from our horses and started climbing down into the ravine gripping the reins for balance.

It wasn't long until we hit the bottom. We searched around but couldn't find another way up on the other side. We decided to follow one of the tunnels through to the other side. "The ceiling of this cave is high we may be faster if we mount our horses" Jack said. So we got back in our saddles and rode into the darkness. I fished a torch out of my pack and lead the way, watching ahead for dangers as far as the torch would allow.

The tunnel was narrow but wide enough to travel single file. We traveled for what felt like hours, but without the view of the sun I couldn't be sure.

I felt a tremor run through the ground and stopped our progress abruptly. "Did you feel that?" I asked. Tom looked back at me with wide eyes, "Maybe it was just a boulder falling in the distance," Jack said nervously.

"Maybe it was the Ender Dragon," Tom whispered in a shaky voice. We didn't need to wait long before we discovered the source of the tremor. Another rumble rang through the tunnel and dust began to fall from the ceiling. The three of us looked up to see blocks of stone shifting as the trembling got more and more aggressive. I was frozen in fear; unable to move when Jack made me spring into action. "RUUUUUN!!!!!" Jack screamed, and we spurred our horses into a gallop as blocks of stone fell around us.

We flew through the tunnel like lighting and came into a large cavern with vaulting ceilings of rock hundreds of blocks high. I didn't have time to marvel at the vastness as blocks continued to fall behind us.

I steered my horse towards an opening to another tunnel in the cavern and just as Tom swept through on his horse blocks slid down and covered the entrance to the tunnel, Jack was still on the other side. This tunnel was wide enough for me to whirl my horse around and the rumbling sounds began to fade as the blocks set into their new places. "JACK!" Tom yelled, as he jumped from his horse. "JACK!" I screamed as I jumped from mine.

Tom and I pounded on blocks of stone but there was no hope in breaking through without a pickaxe. "Did Jack get crushed by the blocks of rock? Did he make it out alive?" These questions ran through my mind as I pounded on the immovable rock.

When my hope for Jack was beginning to fade and Tom was preparing to turn back to his horse, we heard a cough and Jack's voice. "Tom, Steve, I'm okay; the cavern didn't collapse but the tunnel is blocked." "Jack we can get through this wall and get you" I yelled. "No, there is another tunnel, I will follow it out of the mountain" Jack yelled back. "But we need you on this quest Jack!" Tom yelled in sadness, as he stared at the cold flat surface of the rocks. "Go on without me, you will succeed, I believe in you both." Jack mounted his

17

horse, he looked back one last time at the pile of blocks which used to be a tunnel and walked his panting horse to a tunnel leading out of the cavern.

Eventually, after a while of walking in silence, we got out to the other side. "Well isn't this just perfect" Tom said. We had come out of the tunnel right onto a ledge hanging over the side of a massive cliff.

Tom was looking around and eventually called me over. "I found these sticky ropes over here. Maybe we can use them to climb down!" We both agreed that was the only real option without having to turn around. We dismounted and unsaddled our horses. These were mountain horses and would find their own way through the treacherous mountain passes. I started climbing down first, with Tom following right down after me. "UH OH, THE ROPE IS SLIPPING!" Tom yelled out as he clung to the rope. He was clinging to the cliff with one hand to try and keep us from falling, but it wasn't enough. We started falling down towards the ground hundreds, maybe even thousands of blocks down. This was the end for us. Tom and I were going to hit the ground and it would be all over. We weren't going to respawn… I looked down and saw the ground

coming up way too fast. I closed my eyes…
BANG!

I couldn't believe it; I was somehow still alive.
What ever I landed on, it wasn't the ground; it
actually felt a lot like the rope we had tried to use
to climb down the cliff… I slowly opened my
eyes and looked straight into the hundred eyes of
a spider! Tom and I screamed simultaneously. We
looked around and saw hundreds and hundreds of
spiders. We must have landed in the middle of a
massive spider web. We had just survived the
massive fall only to be eaten alive by spiders!

"Relax, the spiders mean you no harm." Said a
voice from somewhere above the spider. "We are
the Spider Riders, do you not recognize us,
Preston?" I craned me neck to get a better look
and saw that there were actually people sitting on
saddles on top of the spiders. "I – I'm not Preston,
I'm his brother. I'm Steve and this is Tom" Tom
could only muster up a small whimper as he
stared wide-eyed at the spider's fangs.

"Can you point us in the direction of the Great
Mountain? I'm actually trying to rescue my
brother from the Huntsmen." I asked of the Spider
Rider leader. "We know all about your brother's
plan. He came through here many months ago on

the same quest." The leader said elegantly, "we will not only point you in the right direction but we shall take you there ourselves!" Without another word Tom and I were picked up by the Spider Riders and thrown on the backs of massive spiders.

We flew through the landscape, as biome after biome blinked past. These spiders were only from the legends. Apparently, they had been given powerful potions to grant them eternal life and incredible speed. Out in the distance the Great Mountain slowly became visible. Slowly, I realized that all around me was the great destruction of the creepers. Entire cities were destroyed. It dawned on me that we were now in the middle of enemy territory; they would most likely attack at any second if they spotted us.

Not even a second after I had that thought I could hear the first cannon fire off their shot. A massive block of TNT flew over my head, singing off some hairs on the top of my head; it struck down a Spider Rider behind me. In the distance, several more cannon shots went off. Almost as fast as the cannons started firing did the Spider Riders pull out their bows and start firing back. One arrow struck a cannon perfectly; the arrow was stuck in the barrel. The cannon tried to fire and the entire structure exploded. One by one each cannon was destroyed in a massive chain reaction, each cannon exploding one after the other.

Just seconds later I realized we had gotten to the base of a giant tree. "Go through the secret entrance at the base of that root and you'll make it into the passage ways under the mountain!" The Spider Rider leader shouted, "We will distract the armies long enough to give you a chance!" With that they were off, the spiders leaping into the distance at full speed.

Tom and I headed straight for the secret entrance; the tunnels were damp, cold, and dark. We shuffled down inside as fast as we could. I didn't want to stay here any longer than I had to. We eventually came to a fork in the tunnel. A sign was pinned up saying, "Left for the jail cells, right for the Chain". I knew I would have to head down to the Chain but Tom could get help from others! "Tom, we need to split up. Go down to the cells and get reinforcements!" I said. "No way man, I'm not going anywhere by myself!" Tom objected. "There's not much time Tom, they'll figure out we're down here soon enough." Tom knew I was right. "Alright" he muttered, "I'll try to hurry and get back to you as soon as I can!"

I gave Tom a quick smile and a nod and started down towards the Chain. I walked for what seemed like several hours before the cave finally started to open up. The room I eventually walked into was massive! I couldn't even see the ceiling. And there it was! The Chain, it was hanging down from the black nothingness above. I worked my way over towards it. Before I knew what was happening, I had slipped and fallen about 30 blocks down. A massive voice boomed behind me "What are you doing down here, little man?" Before I even turned around I knew that it was the Ender Dragon.

I got to my feet and ran towards the Chain at full speed. It was my only hope. I only got half way before I could hear the dragon's wings beat down. He was getting closer and closer with each second. I could feel his fiery hot breath on the back of my neck. If only I had a few more seconds I could just make it to the Chain! But then what? I realized at the last second I didn't actually have a plan for what I would do when I finally got here. With that last thought fresh in my mind the dragon finally caught up to me... He smashed me down and threw my ragged body hundreds of blocks away.

I was amazed that I was even still conscious, but the dragon had knocked my backpack clean off. I looked around and saw it was knocked open on a ledge about 100 blocks below me. But something was wrong - my backpack was glowing! Wait, it wasn't my backpack, it was my grandfathers locket, it was broken in half and glowing. I realized at that moment it wasn't a locket at all - it was an amulet! The Amulet of the Dragon my brother told me about in my dream! That's how I was going to free the dragon and destroy the chain. I had to get down to it.

I looked around and noticed that the dragon was already headed in my direction, I would never make it in time, but I had to try. I began lowering myself over the ledge and heading down. I looked at the dragon and noticed he was only a few dozen blocks away. I knew I only had one shot at this... I had to jump. There was no other way. I only prepared for my leap of faith for a second and then I jumped! I floated through the air and saw the dragon just make it to the spot I was just sitting at. As I was getting closer and closer to the amulet I reached my hand out. I could feel the hot metal of the glowing amulet on my fingers before I clenched my hand and grabbed it.

I didn't waste another second. I spun around while I was still falling and threw the amulet straight at the dragon above me. I hit the ground below not a second after I threw it. I watched the amulet fly towards the dragon, hoping that it would make it. Each second seemed to take an eternity. As it was flying through the air, the amulet seemed like it was growing brighter and brighter. WHAM! It hit the Ender Dragon right in its stomach and I was blinded by the brightest light I had ever seen and, immediately after, deafened by an equally loud BANG. I turned my head around just in time to see the great powerful Chain come down and disintegrate. The shockwave of the explosion reached me, turning everything to black.

My brother was standing over me. Was this another dream? Was everything just a dream? "I can't believe you made it, brother." He said proudly. "I can't believe you saved us all." Tom and Jack were standing on the other side of me. "I got everyone over here as fast as I could. It turned out Jack got himself captured while he was trying to get over here. He was in the jail cells with everyone else!" Tom exclaimed. Preston finally said, "The dragon has been freed! Herobrine and his Huntsmen don't control him any longer! You did it Steve, you did it!"

Preston's expression quickly darkened, though. "Unfortunately, though, the Huntsmen didn't like what we did here today…" he went on ominously; "they struck out and took parts of the homelands".

"That's not even the worst of it. When the dragon was freed, the Huntsmen saw your face, Steve. They know you're the one who has done this to them." I felt my chest tighten as Preston went on. "They are coming for you, and soon you must be ready to face them, for they are on their way!"

Chapter Two – The Great Escape

A pillar slowly appeared right in front of my eyes. I had never seen such a massive city; it was built like a gigantic pillar sticking right up into the bright sky. I could see the different levels and balconies filled with things I couldn't even believe! I thought I could even see the purple shimmer of an Obsidian Gate. The leader of our group of travelers spoke up, "The Great City of Marquis, everyone. It was built way back during the Minecraft Beta Age."

It felt like it had been weeks since I was out building that maze with my best friends, but it had really only been about three days. I was exhausted from everything that had happened since then and I could barely even stay on my horse. My saddle was slowly slipping and I could barely muster up the energy to fix it. I looked over at Jack and saw him slumped over his horse. He was completely passed out! I couldn't believe he was somehow staying on his horse. Tom looked over and we both had a little chucked about it.

We were getting close enough to the city to end up in its far-reaching shadow. I could now see how many people actually lived in this place. There must have been thousands of people going about their day, shopping at the market on the lower levels, sparring at the barracks just outside of the city wall, some even starting their parties in the middle of the afternoon! In fact, the whole city was celebrating. The words of what happened at the great mountain had spread far and wide and the people in the Great city of Marquis were expecting us. They had decorated their entire city with gold and iron blocks and entire rainbows of colorful wool! The entire city was lit up with torches and glowstone. The pillar city looked as if it was on fire, and all of the lights were simply dazzling.

I snapped out of my awe as our horses screeched to a halt. "Stop right there, travelers!" a city guard was walking towards us. "What is your business in the Great City of Marquis?"

"We are the travelers coming out of the Great Mountain! Our band of men here is coming in to enjoy all the festivities the city has to offer. We will be staying here for a few days or weeks and then we are all heading out for the front line of battle!" Commander Hutchinson billowed from on top of his horse. He had been leading the group ever since my brother had to head back to the front line to deal with the rising invasion.

My brother told me all about the enemy we were now facing before he left. He said the Huntsmen had been growing more and more restless ever since the dragon was defeated. Instead of slowing down and falling back like everyone had hoped, the exact opposite was happening. Their attacks became more brutal. More and more creepers were being spawned every day, destroying new parts of our world. Entire sections of the world fell into complete destruction. My brother could only stay with us for one day before he needed to head out. He had learned a lot while he was being held captive, and needed to speak with the consul. He was hoping he could come back and join us in the Great City of Marquis soon. After he rejoined us, we would all go to one of the front line cities. My brother was the only other person that knew about my amulet and how it helped me stop the dragon. He told me that I was one of the few people that could actually use the power that lay inside it. For that very reason I was going to go with him to the front lines! I was supposed to meet some of the greatest fighters of the Greenskeepers.

"Right this way Commander Hutchinson! Right this way!" The city guard led us straight through the entrance and right into a massive market square on the first level of this pillar city. I looked up and immediately thought that the ceiling was far too high! It seemed as if it was hundreds of blocks up, and this was only the first level of the city! The market was filled with hundreds of other people scattered around, busily shopping and buying goods for their families. Emeralds were flying all over the place, buying this, selling that. I had never seen so many people all in one place before. The market back home had only 3 or 4 shops and nothing more! "Look at all of this! I can even see some dragon skin armor!" Jack had finally woken up and noticed where we were. "I'll need to come back down here and beef up on my war supplies!" Tom looked over nervously and hoped that Jack was only kidding. I knew he had seen enough war these past few days for a lifetime!

As soon as we had begun to take it all in, there was a massive boom. I looked around and saw that were was a group of 20-30 soldiers barging in through the front gate. "WE HAVE WOUNDED!" The leading soldier shouted, "MAKE WAY!" It immediately became obvious that very few of the riders were in good shape, some were slumped over their horses and others were trying to keep other riders from falling off their horses.

They must have just come back from a fight with the Huntsmen. That means the enemy must be even closer to the city than I thought. The riders galloped to a building on the other side of the square marked "infirmary". "That does not look good," Tom said. He looked over at me and Jack with his usual nervous glaze. A stranger on the street remarked, "I'm sure they'll be all patched up and healed soon, we have some of the finest medics in all of the land here." I could only hope he was right.

We all got off of our horses and handed them to the barn hands that were waiting for us. They would lead our horses to their own stalls and hitch them up. Next, we headed up to the massive stone staircase on the right side of the market, our crew of men just barely fitting in side by side. "We're stayin' in the Macklemore Inn on the fifth floor, so we got quite a bit o' walkin' to do!" Jeremey Tires said with enthusiasm. He had been excited to see the city ever since he joined our group along with several other soldiers a few days ago.

It took us over 45 minutes to reach the fifth floor, mostly because we had to stop and take a look at everything we saw on each floor on the way up! The festival is going to be amazing when it starts tonight. Finally I saw a sign that read "Macklemore Inn"; it was attached to an old building that looked like it had been here since the very beginning of the city's life. But it had a certain charm to it; the wood almost seemed to glow with wisdom. "We finally have a comfortable place to sleep tonight," I remarked, remembering that last few days of sleeping in makeshift holes in the ground.

The room was much smaller than I expected. It could only just fit 3 beds and a single chest, nothing else. At least it had a window. I looked out and could see all the way to the horizon. The massive green forest that we traveled through to get here was lit up with the setting sun. It almost made me forget about the massive war that was going on. It was almost enough to make the last few days seem like a distant memory.

I looked up to see Jack and Tom packing their gear into the chest. I started packing my things away as well. I decided it would be best to keep my amulet here while we were at the festival! I didn't want to lose it while we were up there.

We had amassed a large amount of armor and weapons over the past few days. The Greenskeepers had very little spare armor and weapons with them so we had to stick with simple wood swords and leather armor. "We should swing by the market and pick up some real weapons tomorrow," Jack said enthusiastically. "Yeah, that and some better armor, this leather can barely protect a fly." I added.

The room was starting to feel a bit musty and I was tired of sitting around and just waiting for the festival to start. After everything that has happened over the last few days, I've been itching for something new and exciting. "Let's go out and do something!" I said eagerly. "Are you crazy?! We only just got here, I think we all deserve a rest." Jack mumbled.

Tom seemed deep in thought, "I think we should try to get as much out of this city while we can. There's a lot of history here, a lot of things to do and see, and besides I could do with a break away from waiting and sitting around for a change." Tom seemed energetic and actually excited to go out and explore. Maybe the past few days had a stronger affect on him than I had imagined.

Jack mumbled some kind of complaint while we were getting ready to go. He slowly started warming up to the idea as we left the room. "Do you think this inn has any secrets?!" He asked excitedly. "Well there's only one way to find out!" I replied. We walked down the hall, passing the doors of other rooms. The last door at the end of the hall was left slightly ajar, and I only just caught a glimpse of something shiny and a tiny bit purple as I walked by. It almost didn't seem real; the way it shined made it look like it was sitting out in the sun and yet we were inside. "Woah! What was that?" I asked, stunned. Tom and Jack quickly looked around and saw the shiny object through the tiny sliver of the opened door.

"That Steve... is our secret!" Jack said eagerly. He headed straight towards the door. "WAIT!" Tom cried, "We shouldn't go in there, we might get in trouble and who knows how dangerous it is!" I guess Tom hadn't changed, and if he had, it wasn't by much! He was still the same old Tom. "A single look can't hurt," I said. Jack didn't need to be told twice, he practically jumped at the door and pulled it back to reveal the giant structure standing right there in the middle of the room. There wasn't much of anything around us, some high walls of red blocks, with the occasional pool of lava taking up a lot of space. We walked around, avoiding any lava by a large margin. Tom was careful to keep the portal in sight at all times, in case we needed to quickly head back. "There! Up ahead!" Tom said with genuine excitement. Jack and I both looked ahead and noticed a tall structure; it almost looked like a grand station. As we got closer and closer I could make out the beautiful stonewalls and pillars. It really was a grand building. The entrance stood dozens of blocks tall.

"Look it says 'The Grand Old Station' right there!" Jack said while pointing just above the massive doorway. "It looks so abandoned and empty," I remarked, I wondered how long ago this station was last used and what kind of station it actually was. I didn't see any Minecart track, and there are no rivers in this place. That gets rid of both Minecart and boats as possibilities. "Well what are we waiting for, let's explore this place.

We have some secrets to discover!" I said with an enthusiastic step towards the entrance.

"We have to be careful, old building like this one are literally falling apart, we have to make sure we don't get crushed in there by any falling blocks!" Tom warned as we passed the first giant pillar outside the entrance. The door was huge and made of the nicest oak wood. It took all of my and Jack's strength to pry it open. Inside was the grandest hall I had ever seen. The ceiling was made of glowstone, white stone, and even diamond lights! The walls were made of the same materials and grand pillars were spread out across the room. There were hundreds of hallways coming off the main room each with their own sign above the door.

"What is this place?!" Jack asked with awe, "I've never seen any station like this. The one back home is nothing more than a single Minecart track." Tom started walking and looking around, inspecting everything he could. "I think this place might be a Nether Portal Station. There appear to be portals down each of these hallways, all leading to different areas in the kingdom. You could reach any part of the world with this station!" Tom said quickly and excitedly.

"Well it looks completely abandoned, I don't think any of these portals are even on right now." Jack observed. "They must have shut them all down for the war then, incase anyone was ever going to use them to bomb cities or worse…" I concluded. Tom looked extremely nervous all of a sudden, "Wait a minute… did you guys hear that?!" Jack and I both looked at each other with a confused stare, "Hear what?" We both said in unison. "RUNNNN!" Tom screamed at us as he started sprinting towards the entrance.

Jack and I quickly followed behind him; we still had no idea what we were running from. As soon as we got outside I immediately noticed what had set Tom off. There were hundred of zombie pigmen and dozens of ghasts flying overhead. We all grinded to a halt as we took in just how many enemies there were… "WE HAVE TO GET BACK TO THE PORTAL!" I screamed, "Before they notice us!" No one needed to be told twice as we too off in a dead sprint back to the portal.

We easily got about halfway back without any problem; nothing had noticed us in the crowd of enemies. It seemed like we could make it back unscathed. Jack and I exchanged a nervous but optimistic glance as we kept moving through the horde, trying to find the safest and fastest path back to the portal... Where did all these things comes from?!

I heard a shriek come from the sky; it was a horrible high-pitched squeal. Before I could even look up to see the ghast, he fired off his fireball. It flew towards us at full speed, smashing down only a few blocks away. "GO! GO! GO!" Jack yelled. The commotion got everey enemies attention on us, I could see distant ghasts moving closer, the zombie pigmen turned hostile as a few of their own were killed in the explosion.

The portal was still a bit away but we could make it if we kept up our speed. Tom was running faster than I had ever seen him run and Jack was right on his tail. Another fireball was fired off as we started nearing the portal, it smashed the pillar of the portal and turned off the portal's purple shimmer. "NOOOO!" Tom screamed as he realized we were trapped here.

"We need a flint and steel right now!" Tom said without skipping a beat. He placed down a crafting table before Jack and I could even respond. I quickly looked in my backpack to see if I had the necessary items. I looked and looked and finally I found an iron ingot and a piece of old flint, I handled them to Tom and he built a flint and steel instantly. "Let's go!" he yelled as he relit the portal and jumped on.

We were back in the safety of the inn before we knew it. "That was way too close…" Tom muttered. There were no monsters were shooting at us here, we were completely safe again. We quietly walked back to our room and slumped down on our beds. We were fast asleep in seconds.

"Time to head out! The party is on the top floor of the city!" Commander Hutchinson just poked his head into our room long enough to remind us before he was off again. The festival was going to go on for a full 10 days and it started tonight. It was supposed to be one of the biggest of its kind in the entire world. "Let's get going guys!" Tom excitedly said, "I wonder if we'll get to see the great Villagers of Marquis! They're rumored to only come out for the festival."

We left our room and started walking down the stairs towards the exit of the inn. The entire inn was filled with travelers from all over the world. Some of them looked just as terrifying as the enemy we had faced in the woods, the pickpockets and bandits that had made up the darker side of the forest. Others looked a lot friendlier. Some of these people could have been from my own village; they must have come up here for the festival.

One woman was talking to the three other women at her table, "I really hope this festival is all it's hyped up to be. I could really use some fun and happiness during these dark and dreary days." The women all agreed with that. All of a sudden one of them looked over at me, "Hey aren't you that boy?! The one that took out the dragon!" I was taken by surprise, did people actually know who I was?! "I... I, yeah that was me" I said, not knowing what to say. "Well thank you, we all thank you," she replied. "You're... You're welcome." I still couldn't believe I was responsible for that; it was going to take some getting used to.

"We gon' take the escalator this time boys."
Hutchinson said. "An escalator? … " Tom said,
"What?" "Don't tell me you've never used an
escalator? Hutchinson asked with his signature
accent, "Well it's jus' like a regular old staircase
but with some Redstone wire thrown in to make
the stairs move for ya! All you gotta do is stand
on them and wait to get to the top!" Hutchinson
explained excitedly, "You'll see 'em in just a
sec'."

We walked through the city streets past the older
district and came right up to the escalator - it sure
was something to see! I had never seen redstone at
work like this before. A row of stairs four blocks
wide moved up towards the next level of the city
all automatically. I could see a complex system of
pistons and redstone wire work tirelessly, moving
together in time and in sync. It was amazing. I
was a little nervous to get on but Jack ran up
ahead and jumped on as fast as he could. Tom and
I both followed after him and jumped on too.

The entire ride up these moving stairs was just
something else. It was simply amazing, but it
didn't' seem like too many other people were
impressed. They must have been completely used
to using this thing. After a few minutes we
stepped out on the top floor of the city! I could see

the night sky appear above me. The sun was just setting and the stars had started to come out. The party had already started. There were thousands of people walking around. I heard a huge swell of music and cheering coming from the far side of the pillar. Each building up here seemed like it was built just for the festival. There were restaurants, music halls, party tents, and there was even a massive glass area built over the side of the pillar. "Meet us back down at the ol' inn in about three hours and we can keep the festival goin' down there!" Hutchinson said to us right as he took off towards the nearest restaurant.

I headed over to the glass overhang and stood on top of it. I saw all the way down to the ground. I could just barely make out the road that we came in on. It must have been several hundred blocks down. I couldn't believe that such a massive city even existed. I wondered if it had taken hundreds of years to build such a city.

"LET THE FESTIVAL BEGIN!" A voice billowed over the entire city. The crowds of people erupted into cheers and screams. As the yelling died down, it was replaced by some of the best music I had ever heard. I looked around to see where it was coming from and saw a band of villagers playing on some jukeboxes. "Check it out Tom, there are some of those villagers you were talking about!" I said, "No way! Let's get over there." Tom said as he started walking towards them.

They looked even cooler up close. The villagers had been a very rare mob ever since the players took over the world hundreds of years ago. I had never actually seen them besides in old pictures and books. The music they were playing was just as rare. There were only a few true records left, as no one knew how to craft them. They could only be found in dungeons hundreds of years ago. The villagers were some of the few people who still had copies of the music. Oh if only my brother could be here and hear this music! I hoped that he would get here soon.

"Let's get some food! Then we can check out the fireworks!" Jack was looking at all the different places that offered food and I saw how excited he was to try it all. We decided to have some cake, followed by a very thin slice of golden apple. "Wow, what meal," I said with a full stomach. In the distance I could hear the very first firework fly up into the sky and explode. I looked behind me just in time to see a huge explosion of color and light. It lit up the entire area!

We all got up and quickly tried to find a better place to watch the fire works. We settled on a big rock just outside one of the restaurants. We were overlooking the main square where they were setting off all of the fire works. Explosion after explosion went up and lit the entire area. Every once in a while 10 or 20 fireworks were launched all at once and exploded, creating a huge wave of light that washed over all of us. The crowds cheered every time one of them went off. The music was still going on in the background. So far, the festival was going extremely well.

"Steve, is it? Your brother sent me to find you!" An old man was whispering something in my ear.

My friends didn't even notice he was there. "This place isn't safe anymore; you need to leave this city and head for the last safe place, the forest of Oceania." "What are you talking about? Who are you?!" I said stunned by what he was saying. "There is NO TIME!" the old man said, "I will explain everything as soon as we are safe!"

Before this strange old man said another word a massive explosion rocked the top floor of the city. People all around seemed confused; no one was sure if a firework has misfired or if it was something else. BOOOOOM, another explosion shook the entire top floor, this time there was no mistaking it for an attack. People everywhere started screaming. I was knocked down to the ground before I could even hear the next explosion. I looked to the horizon and saw a massive fireball coming right for the top floor of the building. The old man saw it too and braced himself. He held his hands together and muttered some words under his breath. Before I knew what was happening he shouted at the top of his lungs and threw his hands towards the incoming fireball. A vast green light had shot out and struck the fireball off center; the fireball was blown off course and only took out a small section of the pillar instead of smashing directly into it.

I could just scramble to my feet before I saw the next fireball fly towards the city. The old man started mumbling to himself and closed his eyes. This time he struck the fireball head on. The fireball shattered into a thousand pieces. The old man looked right at me and shouted, "Get out of here! Get out of here now, I'll try to keep the city from collapsing!" His voice was drowned out by a nearby explosion. All I could hear was a high-pitched whine. I looked around and found Tom lying on the ground. Jack and I helped him to his feet. I looked at both of them and they knew that we needed to get out of here right away. We sprinted back towards the escalator, but the massive crowds of people were all trying to cram onto it at once. It wasn't even worth trying.

There had to be another way down to the bottom. Tom spoke up and I just barely heard him over the high-pitched whine, "We can use the maintenance shaft! I read about them last year!" "Okay, lead the way!" I shouted. Tom ran out ahead straight away from the crowds of people. We had to run to the complete other side of the pillar. Finally we saw a little building dug in between two larger buildings. The sign on the door said "Maintenance: No Entrance!" Jack ran up to the door and kicked it in without skipping a beat. We all ran inside and went straight down the ladder. I was on my way down when I realized there were hundreds of blocks of empty space underneath us! A single slip up here would have been really bad. We slowly worked our way down, every few seconds an explosion erupted above us and I griped the rungs of the ladder as hard as I could. I knew that the old man on the top floor was still holding off the massive fireballs, as all the explosions so far had been nothing more than TNT blocks. I only hoped that he could keep them off until we were able to leave the city.

We were almost all of the way down when the first fireball struck the building. There was a mammoth explosion way above us. The entire city rocked back and forth, swaying with the force of the impact. I gripped the ladder as hard as I could but it was no use. The ladder broke free from the wall and I was going down with it. I knew we were at least 30 or 40 blocks above the ground floor. I closed my eyes and braced for impact. I felt the wind whipping my face as I sped towards the ground.

"OOF". All of the wind was knocked out of my lungs and my leg was smashed against something, hard. Pain shot through my entire body as I tried to stand up. As soon as I put some weight on my leg, I fell back down and almost passed out from the pain. I looked around and saw that a market stall broke my fall. I must have fallen on the soft cloth of the roof, but my leg hit the wooden support beam. I closed my eyes to deal with the pain. Jack shook me and my eyes shot right open, as he had finally made it down the ladder. "Tom is hurt bad we need to get him out of here! Can you stand?" He asked. "I can try again but my leg is wounded." I replied. I tried getting up again careful not to put any weight on my bad leg. I only just did it through the pain, but I was standing.

I hobbled over to where Jack was standing. "He fell straight onto the ground. There was nothing to break his fall." Jack explained. I looked down at Tom, "Tom, we have to get out of here. We'll have to carry you out!" I only heard a mumbled reply but we didn't have time to figure out what he was saying. "We're going to need horses!" I told Jack, he nodded in agreement and ran off towards the stables. I sat down next to Tom, taking the weight off my injured leg, "We're going to get out of here. Jack should be back with the horses any second."

I heard the second fireball only milliseconds before it struck the city, and this time it hit much closer than before. I looked up at the massive fireball right as it broke through the ceiling. It must have hit the second level! It crushed through the ceiling and smashed down right in the middle of the market, skidding to a halt right as it broke through the wall on the other side of the building. This fireball had weakened the support beams that were spread throughout the market. Those beams kept the building standing! The entire structure was creaking and the building was slowly swaying side to side. I got sick just thinking about how much of the city was sitting above us on half broken supports.

Jack was sprinting back to us. He had three horses following behind him. He looked extremely panicked. "WE HAVE TO GO! NOW!" He shouted, "THE WHOLE THING IS GOING TO COME DOWN!" I looked around and knew he was right; the fireballs had done too much damage. I got to my feet as quickly as I could with my hurt leg. I reached down and picked up Tom with Jacks help. We just got him on to his horse. Jack strapped him in as best as I could as I slowly got on top of my horse.

Slowly, I realized with horror that my amulet was still upstairs in that chest! Oh my goodness I could not lose that amulet! It had been passed down for generations! If the city went down so does the amulet… I only panicked for another second before Jack said "What are you waiting for!? Let's go!"

"CREEPERS INCOMING!" A guard shouted right as he opened fire with his bow. A huge explosion took out a part of the wall near the entrance just seconds later. It wasn't going to be easy escaping from this building. I spurred my horse and shouted, "Let's get go!" Jack spurred his horse and kicked off, too. Tom's horse was tied to Jack's, and quickly followed along. We rode our horses between the stalls, going as fast as we could. The ceiling was creaking dangerously. It echoed throughout the entire market. This ceiling was just about ready to collapse. I spurred my horse faster and faster, and my horse was giving it all it had. I could finally see the exit coming up in front of us. It was only another minute of galloping before we reached it.

The third fireball came in even faster than the previous two. I heard it wreck the city above me. The explosion reverberated through every last bit of the building. Support blocks began raining from the ceiling. I tried my best to dodge them on my horse as they came flying down. A massive 15-block support beam crashed down just a few blocks ahead of me. I tried everything I could to turn my horse in time but it was no use. I smashed straight into the beam and flew off my horse to the other side of the fallen beam. I closed my eyes to try to block out the pain in my leg but it was no use. I had to get up and get back to my horse before the whole building came down. I whistled to my horse, urging him to come closer. I grabbed ahold of his reins as soon as I could, slowly pulling myself up. It was time-consuming, but it was working. A massive whip like crack shot from one side of the ceiling straight across to the other side. It was instantly followed by the beginning of the collapse of the entire city.

Jack made his way around the support beam and came right up to me and lifted me the last bit up onto my horse, "WE HAVE TO GET OUT

NOW!" I looked at the exit straight on and spurred my horse like it was the end of the world. Both my and Jack's horses were galloping as fast as they could. With each stride we got a little closer to that exit. With each stride we were a little closer to making it out of here in one piece. Tom's horse was working as hard as he could, too – I was glad to see that Tom was still strapped in properly.

A huge support beam smashed down in front of us again. This time it was further away so we had some time to react. I steered around it, just clipping the corner of the beam but nothing more. From here it was only 20 blocks until we were at the exit. A huge explosion ripped through the ceiling. It seemed like yet another fireball had struck at the core of the building! What happened to that old man? Was he not able to hold them off anymore?!

I didn't have another second to think as the roof started coming down. At first it came down slowly, small sections of building and houses from the second floor crashing down. Thankfully, it started on the other side of the city, far away from us. But it was coming closer and closer and fast! Right as we made it through the exit I heard a massive rumble and the largest explosion I've ever heard right behind us. I knew the entire city was coming down. I rode my horse as fast I possible, I did not want to be hit by falling rumble. I heard explosion after explosion as the city crumbled down; there was a deep rumble as the city was collapsing. We rode at full speed for about 200 blocks before we thought it was safe. Finally I looked back and saw the final piece of the building collapse in on its self. The once great city was now nothing more than a pile of blocks. I slumped over my horse, exhausted.

"We made it man…" Jack said tiredly. I closed my eyes for just a second as I tried to let my body relax. I felt a dull throb in my hurt leg. I thought about my now lost amulet, wondering if I could ever get it back. I slowly opened my eyes when yet another explosion went off not 20 blocks away from us. I looked around and realized that we were not out of the danger yet. We ran out of the dangers of the building just to run into a war zone!

Creepers were walking around everywhere I looked. There were Greenskeeper soldiers everywhere, trying to diffuse the creepers and destroy them without setting them off. Not very many were succeeding. There was another explosion far too close for comfort. The shockwave had my horse reeling in panic. I tried to calm him down as I yelled to Jack, "We have to head for the hills! Get to higher ground!" He nodded back at me as he adjusted his reins. We took off as fast as we could. Our horses were getting tired. They wouldn't be able to keep this pace up for much longer.

I saw a creeper ahead of me in my path coming up on my right. I banked hard to the left, trying to stay clear of him. I couldn't get out of the way in time… I was going to get too close. Right as the creeper was about to explode, a single arrow flew through the sky and hit the creeper right in his back. The creeper disappeared and a small piece of gunpowder landed on the ground in his place. I had no time to consider how lucky I was before an explosion ripped through a nearby tree. A block of wood flew right past my head, whizzing by. I pushed my horse to full speed, heading straight to the top of the hill. We were almost at the top, "We should head into the forest! The old man said something about a forest being safe!" I shouted over the explosions. Our horses came to a stop as we looked around, trying to figure out what direction we should go in. "There's no point heading back into the forest we came from… Over there!" Jack pointed to a forest several hundred blocks in the direction opposite of the way we came. "Alright let's go!" We took off again.

We rode and rode, dodging creepers as we went, weaving through ranks of Greenskeeper soldiers fighting them. The trees grew closer and closer together. I caught a glimpse of the night sky as we rode and saw hundred of tiny little lights flying across it. It took me a second to realize that those were blocks of TNT coming down straight towards the entire battlefield. "INCOMING!" I shouted right as the TNT made contact with the ground. Each explosion shredded and tore through the battlefield. An explosion went off right next to my horse and me. The power from the explosion threw me right off my horse and straight onto the ground. I couldn't hear a thing; my ears must have been affected by the explosion - but I still felt the vibrations from the explosions around me. I was lying on my back and saw hundreds of lights appear in the sky yet again. Before I knew what was happening the entire ground erupted in an earthquake of explosions. This time I was lucky enough not to be that close to any of them. Time seemed to slow down. It all seemed so surreal. As I tried to get up I was surprised that I could barely feel the pain in my leg. The adrenaline must have blocked out the pain. I looked around, trying to find my friends, as I was knocked to the ground by another explosion.

I got up again, trying once more to find my friends in all the rubble around me. My hearing came back rapidly and all of a sudden I heard shouting, "STEVE! RUN!" I didn't know where the shouting came from or who had said it but I listened and ran as hard as I could. I caught sight of my friends on their horses as I sprinted. A huge explosion went off behind me where I had been standing just a few seconds ago. My friends had my horse with them; he must have avoided a lot of the explosions. I saw that Jack was covered in mud; he was probably thrown off of his horse during the rain of TNT, too.

We were much closer to the tree line than I thought we were, only about a hundred blocks out. I ran up to my horse and jumped on. We rode our horses even faster and harder than before. We were so close to making it off the battlefield and into the forest. I noticed the night sky light up with TNT one last time, "NOT AGAIN, HOLD ON!" I screamed as the TNT rained down. This time we weren't so lucky. The TNT exploded right between all of us. I had no chance of staying on my horse. I was knocked down to the ground right as another block of TNT went off nearby. I looked up just in time to see Tom fall of his horse. Not a second later, our horses were spooked by another explosion and spirited off, "NO, WAIT, COME BACK HERE!" I shouted after them, but it was no use.

I slowly got back to my feet, surprised that the explosion didn't hurt us more than it did. Tom was still wounded from his fall but other than that he didn't seem any worse for wear. "Are you able to walk, Tom?" Jack asked, all he got in reply was some mumbling. Jack looked over at me and said, "We'll have to carry him as far as we can. How's your leg?" I replied with "It's alright. It hurts, but I should be able to help out."

I pulled Tom to his feet with Jack and we both supported him under each of his arms. We were able to walk fairly quickly towards the trees.

"Here's to hoping we get off this forsaken battlefield before the next wave of TNT arrives," I said. The tree line was steadily getting closer, and we passed our first tree right as I saw the night sky light up again. "Hurry!" I shouted as we picked up the pace. The TNT could have struck down any second.

The tree line was just blocks away at this point and we started running as fast as we could while supporting Tom. "WE MADE IT!" Jack shouted as we crossed the barrier into the woods. Whatever Jack said next was drowned out by the sound of TNT smashing down and exploding behind us. "We need to keep going," Jack repeated, "We have to get as far away as we can."

We moved further into the forest, the leaves and branches slowly blocked out the far away sounds of battle. Slowly the explosions sounded no louder than the snapping branches under our feet. Finally, after we had made it a far way into the forest, the sound of battle disappeared entirely. All that was left was the quiet hum of the forest. I could hear animals just out of sight; somewhere off in the distance there was a pack of howling wolves. I looked up and saw a lot of bats flying overhead.

The forest was extremely dark, and every step in was darker than the step before it. We had no idea what direction we should be heading in, so all we could do was keep moving forward.

Eventually the ground started sloping up. Soon we were hiking up a tall hill. We finally reached the top and saw that the other side of the hill sloped down into a grassy field. The forest continued just past this little field. "Look! What is that?" Jack said, pointing down into the grassy field. "I have no idea… Wait a minute, are those spiders?!" I replied. Sure enough the entire field was covered in spiders going about their lives.

"What should we do?" Jack asked, "We can't just go running through a field of spiders, especially not with Tom." "We'll have to go around." I said, "There's nothing else we can do." We set off and stuck to the trees as much as we could. Eventually, we were slowly walking around the field.

I saw a spider rustle right past us but he must have just not seen us. I kept an eye on the field the entire time we went around. The moon came out from behind a cloud and lit up the grassy field. There were hundreds and hundreds of spiders walking around, some of them fighting between each other, and others just basking in the night skylight. We started walking faster as we finally made it around the field. Finally, the field was out of sight and safely behind us.

After a few minutes we finally stopped moving and took a break to catch our breath. "We are not getting off easy tonight!" I said. "You can say that again," Jack replied, "We need to find a place to rest, I don't think I can carry Tom for much longer." "Yeah, me neither. We'll have to keep going until we find something..." I hoped that we would find something soon.

The adrenaline from the battle had completely worn off and I was feeling exhausted, the dull pain in my leg growing sharp. Every step now shot pain up my entire body. "I don't think I'll be able to make it much further" I told Jack a few minutes later.

The pain was only getting worse. We had to find something soon or we would be stranded in these woods at night. "Do you see that? Or am I just going crazy?" Jack asked. "What?" I replied, unsure of what he was talking about. "Right over there. Is that some kind of door underneath those bushes?" Jack sounded unsure of himself. We started walking in the direction he had mentioned. I still couldn't see what he was going on about; all I saw were some bushes in between the trees. "Hold Tom here for a minute," Jack walked up to the bushes and used his signature kick to break open a door that instantly appeared out of nowhere. I could see a massive space inside the doorway; there was furniture and a kitchen, and even a crafting room! But I couldn't even see a trace of this house outside before Jack kicked the door in; it was as if it was invisible. "How did you see that?!" I asked, incredibly impressed. "I don't know. I just looked over and saw a simmer of something…" Jack didn't seem like he knew how he had spotted the invisible door, but he did and that's all the mattered now! "Let's get inside." I said without skipping a beat.

The house was massive. It seemed like it was built hundreds of years ago and just abandoned by the original owners. Maybe they had lost track of where they built it. "I bet Tom would know something about this house. He always seems to know something about everything," I remarked.

We carried Tom over to one of the beds. Hopefully he would feel better once he had a full nights rest. If he didn't, we'd have to find some way of making a health potion in this house. Maybe there was some kind of storeroom filled with everything that we need and this house looked like it held a lot of secrets.

The house seemed like it was once a castle or part of an older kingdom, the decorations were all ancient and there was no redstone what so ever. There were a lot of bedrooms and even more hallways. "I don't think I'll be able to stay awake for another minute." Jack yawned. "I hear you. I don't think I can either" I said. "Goodnight Steve" Jack mumbled before walking into one of the bedroom. I did the same, I looked out the window for a split second before getting into bed and I saw the rising sun. We had been awake for the whole night. I got into bed and closed my eyes. My throbbing leg acted as a constant reminder of what had happened during the night. Slowly I fell into a dreamless sleep.

Chapter Three – The Death Raiders

I was woken up by a loud thump. It came from somewhere else in the house. I scrambled to get out of my bed but as soon as I stood up my weight collapsed under my leg. The pain had gotten much worse; I could barely get back up, even while supporting myself on the bed. I head another thump; it was getting closer to my room. "Jack? Is that you?" I called out. It was coming closer and closer. I did all I could to try and get back up to my feet. I would need to be standing if I wanted a fighting chance. I saw a chair in the corner…Perfect! I used that to balance myself.

Finally the thumping was right outside my door. Whoever it was, they were coming in. I didn't even have a sword on me. I would have to use my fists if it came to a fight. As the door opened I immediately recognized who it was. It was the old man from the festival, the wizard who tried to hold off the fireballs from hitting the city! "Hello there," he said, "I hope I didn't frighten you! That was not my intention." I couldn't believe he was here, how did he find us… "How did you find us here?" I asked, confused. He chucked and replied

"How did I find you? How did you find my house!?" I couldn't believe it, this was his house? How was that even possible?

"Come. I'll explain everything I know in the living room, Jack is already awake. Tom is still sleeping. I gave him some health potion as soon as I got here - he should be completely fine within a few days or weeks depending on how injured he was." The old man explained. We started walking out of my room; I was still using the chair to balance myself. The old man saw me and said, "Here, use my cane. It should be much better than using a chair!" I took his cane from him. As soon as I touched the wood I felt something beneath my fingers, as if the wood was somehow charged. The old man shot me a knowing smile before we started walking again.

He turned around once more, right before he left my room, "You didn't happen to misplace this?" He said with a smile as he took out my amulet from under his cloak. "You found it! I can't believe it… Thank you so much! I thought I had lost it forever in the rubble of the city." I said with a massive smile on my face. "I think you'll need it soon enough, so I thought it might have been worth retrieving," the old man said and with that we headed downstairs.

"Good mornin'! I got started on breakfast, I hope you don't mind!" Jack said with a piece of bacon in his hand.

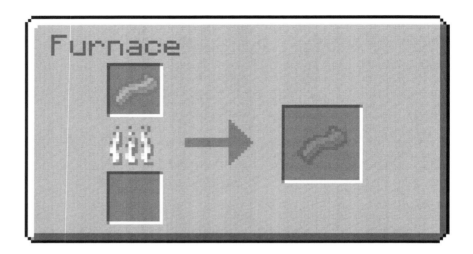

"Did you hear the good news about Tom?" I nodded to acknowledge that I had. We all sat down and I grabbed a piece of bacon of my own. "I don't even know your name," I said to the old man. "My name is Tristan, Tristan The Wise," the old man said, "I am a wizard from the olden days, the days before the Huntsmen even existed." The old man took a deep sip from his mug before continuing. "I don't know how the Huntsmen pulled off that sneak attack on the Great City of Marquis..." His voice trailed off. There was a deep look of sadness in his eyes, "The city was hundreds of miles away from the front lines.

Herobrine must have led the Huntsmen around every defense we had in place."

"It doesn't spell good news for the war, I can tell you that," the wizard went on, "But enough of the bad news! How did you ever find this house? I thought I had cast my spell of invisibility properly!" I looked over at Jack and said, "Jack said he saw a shimmer in the distance, I couldn't see anything, but once we got closer he saw it was the entrance to the house. I don't know how he found it." The wizard lifted an eyebrow as he looked over at Jack, "Is that so?" Jack just shrugged his shoulders and kept on eating his breakfast.

"Well in any case, it's lucky you found this place, the Huntsmen have been searching through this forest all day." Tristan went on, "They know who you are Steve, and they know you're the one who took down the dragon." The wizard took another long sip from his mug, "That dragon was one of their strongest weapons. It was really brave what you did, but unfortunately it wasn't enough to end this war." I still couldn't believe that I had done all that, every day it seems more like a dream. "You said that my brother sent you?" I asked, "Do you know him?" The wizard replied, "As yes, your brother had realized that there might be an attack at the Great City of Marquis. He had pieced together what he learned in the Great Mountain just in time."

"It was good that he sent you, I'm not sure that we would have made it out of that city alive without your help." I told Tristan. He nodded his head in understanding. "Listen, your brother told me about the amulet, he told me what you could do with it," the wizard's expression became very serious, "that amulet is the secret to winning this war. The amulet is from the first beta age, when the great wizards that came even before me crafted it. The flames of the dragon you defeated smelted it, and some of his power now resides in that amulet."

"I will tell you more as time goes on," Tristan said, "But for now we should rest and gain our strength back." And with that the wizard stood up and walked up the stairs toward the bedrooms. I was more than tired myself and this breakfast wasn't helping. I started a fire in the fireplace, sat back down in front of it, put my feet up, and went back to sleep.

I slowly opened my eyes. I realized I must have been asleep for several hours. My fire had died out and all that was left was ash in its place. I walked around the house with Tristan's cane and found Jack awake in the kitchen; he was making what I assumed was the next mornings breakfast. "Good morning to ya!" he said, "You slept through an entire day Steve! You musta been tired. Tristan left early this morning. He said that he would be back in a few days' time." I didn't expect him to leave so soon! "Did he say where he was going?" I asked. Jack replied, "No he just told he would be back in a few days and that's it, nothing else." He shrugged his shoulders and went back to cooking up some bacon, "Tom is still sleeping, and I'm hoping he will wake up by the end of the week. I don't know how he survived that fall straight to the ground - he's one lucky guy."

I spent all day fading in and out of sleep, my leg still throbbing and my body still aching with pain. The other night played through my dreams, the constant explosions while running down the battlefield periodically woke me up from my slumber. I still remember how scared I was running away from the city. I don't know how we were so lucky to make it out of there together and in one piece. I kept dreaming about the dragon and my amulet. How did my family get ahold of such a powerful object? I'm sure we just passed it

down father to son. I drifted back into sleep
before I could think of a reasonable answer.

Just like that another day passed. I didn't even wake up for the breakfast the next morning. By the time I rolled out of bed and hobbled down stairs I was just in time for lunch. "You sure love cooking, Jack. I don't think I've even made a single thing since we got here." I remarked. "Haha you got that right! There's nothing I like more than making and eating food!" Jack said with a laugh. It looked like he had made some mushroom soup. I grabbed a bowl and dug in. "This is really good!" I said, complimenting Jack's cooking skills, "So has anything new happened? Is Tristan back yet?" I asked. Jack just shook his head, "No, nothing exciting has happened in ages! I haven't even seen one of those Huntsmen out searching for us."

The sun had just set and I was feeling more awake than I had been for the past few days, it must have been something in the lunch Jack made. I just knew I wouldn't be able to fall sleep anytime soon. Instead of heading up to my room like Jack, I decided to explore the house a bit. I had barely seen any of this place in the time I had spent here.

The bedrooms on the top floor all seemed the same; they had the same furniture and the same layout. I only noticed small changes, a different painting here, a new bed there. I slowly limped through each doorway taking a quick glace before moving on to the next room.

I was starting to get bored of exploring right as I noticed something was off about the last room I walked by. There was something else on the wall here that I didn't see in any of the other rooms. A lone torch was sitting on the wall. It would have never seemed out of place if I hadn't been paying attention to the pattern and design of each room before it.

As I got closer to the torch I could see it wasn't like any of the other torches in the house. There was something else… it looked as if the torch was placed on something. I only got another second of inspecting it before my hurt leg gave out underneath me.

I thrashed out my arms in panic as I fell to the ground. My hand grabbed onto the base of the torch just in time to steady myself. Before I knew what was happening the torch gave away and slid away from the wall. I looked up as I got my balance back and saw that the torch had pulled out whatever it was attached to.

Only a split second later the wall behind the torch groaned and I could hear the distinct clicking of pistons as they worked. For I few moments all I could hear was the mechanical clicks behind the wall. Finally the blocks of the wall started to move back as the pistons moved the blocks out of the way. As everything settled down and the pistons slowed the wall had turned into a dark looking walkway.

I knew this house had plenty of secrets but I wasn't expecting to find one of them so quickly! I excitedly grabbed the torch off the wall and made my way down the tunnel. At first it seemed as if it went on forever straight out from the room but I quickly realized the tunnel was slowly starting to turn to the left. I was walking as quickly as I could manage on my leg, holding the wall with one hand for support.

"How can this tunnel still be going to the left?!" I asked myself, entirely confused. The tunnel had been turning left for much longer than I though was possible, I should have come around full circle by now and hit the tunnel I had come from! As unreal as it seemed the tunnel just continued on, going left. I had been walking for a while, it was starting to seem like I was going in circles.

I turned around and started going back, this tunnel was bad news, and it didn't seem natural. I had a heavy feeling as I started walking back, soon it seemed as if the tunnel was starting to turn left yet again. I couldn't believe it! Soon I started getting confused on which way was which, I didn't know if I had already come back this way or if I hadn't seen this tunnel yet. I turned around again only to turn around one more time. I started getting panicked as I realized I might be trapped in these windy tunnels.

I started losing track of time. I decided I needed to stop turning around and head in only one direction. By now I knew these tunnels were playing tricks on me. I could only imagine where they were taking me.

The tunnel was finally straightening out. I started to notice a faint glow on the blocks in front of me. I slowly started speeding up my walk as the glow got stronger and stronger. The tunnel began growing wider and wider as I walked on, the ceiling started to climb up and up. Eventually I was in a tall and dark room the size of a full house.

I never realized all of this could fit into the place was had been staying! I came to the realization that this entire section of the building must have been built using the strongest of magic or at the very least an extremely complicated redstone wire system.

I walked down the tall and wide room in the dark with only my torch to guide me. Things had finally seemed to return to normal. The walls weren't changing and I didn't feel like I was losing my mind again.

A sudden and sharp burst of white light appeared right in front of me. Just like that the strange weird magic from before had returned. The floor I was standing on began to shift under my feet. Before I knew it the light from just a second ago went out along with my torch!

In the darkness the blocks under me were still shifting. They were forming a slope. I started sliding towards the other side of the room, away from where I had come in. The floor only got more and more steep as time went on. I started speeding up and soon I was practically falling straight down.

I slammed into the ground as hard as I possibly could. Pain shot through my entire body as I slowly tried to stand up. For a split second I though I had reinjured my hurt leg, but the pain only lasted for a moment before it passed. My body was still aching as I got back on my feet.

The area I was standing in was well lit. I looked up but only saw a ceiling, it seemed that wherever I had come from was no longer there. "This was just a bad idea…" I mumbled to myself as I started walking forward.

There was another passageway up ahead. The stone walls seemed to close in on me as I walked forward, I started feeling claustrophobic. Soon I was down to a single block of space, nothing more. It felt like being back in the old mines I used to play in with Tom and Jack back home only this time I was alone.

I heard a rumble behind me, it sounded as if it were only a few dozen blocks away. I started to limp faster and faster. I could feel my leg stiffen as I sped up. By the time I heard the second rumble I was running as fast as I could. Whatever was making that sound was starting to gain on me. By now it was only around 10 blocks or so behind me. I gave myself as extra push and started sprinting; my limp leg was barely slowing me down.

I smashed straight through the blocks in front of me. They had come out of nowhere and had broken into pieces as if they were made of glass. I was confused and had completely forgotten about being chased for a moment as I looked around. It seemed as if I was somehow now outside, out in a small grassy field. In the middle of the day, with the sun right above me even though it was the middle of the night! There was no sign of any tunnels, the forest, or even the house! Whatever had been chasing me was nowhere to be found.

I closed my eyes for a moment. I was regretting my decision to ever enter that hidden tunnel in the first place. I just stood there for a while, thinking about how any of this was even possible. Had I somehow teleported to this field? I couldn't have just stepped from inside a tunnel to the middle of a grassy field. That's just impossible!

After I thought about it for a while and couldn't figure out how any of this was happening. I decided to move on. I was going to head out to the only tree on the horizon, the only visible landmark in this place.

As I got to the tree I instantly knew it was the right thing to do, there was a trapdoor at the base of the tree. Without even thinking about it I opened the trap door and went down. I climbed and climbed and finally dropped off at the bottom. I couldn't believe it! It was the same windy tunnel from the start of all this exploring!

Only this time there was something different. I couldn't put my find on exactly what it was but I started walking down the tunnel with confidence. It felt as if I had mastered this tunnel's games and it simply couldn't mess with me any longer.

Before too long the tunnel started straightening out. I could see the very entrance I had come in from. I started speeding up but it seemed as if this tunnel had one last idea for me. I instantly dropped down several blocks as the tunnel floor gave away. I was starting to really get tired of this. I had dealt with enough for one night.

But as I looked up I realized this wasn't another one of these silly mind games. No instead there was a huge library standing in front of me. It was filled with thousands and thousands of books! In the middle there was a single huge leather bound book sitting on it's own display table. I went up to it and saw that it must have been Tristan's very own book on magic! It was filled with spells, the history of magic and other things I couldn't even believe! It talked about the ancient magical defenses put into place to protect this library and everything it held.

Soon I read down to a part talking about the powerful sleeping enchantments place down inside the library itself. Apparently anyone who stood in the library long enough would become inexplicably tired and simply forget how he ever got there in the morning and soon they would forget the library ever existed.

I laughed out loud when I read this. "I'm not even feeling a little bit drossy," I thought to myself. I looked up from the book and could just out of the corner of my eye see the bedroom I had come in from. For some strange reason I had a strong desire to walk over to the bed. "I suppose it would be wise to continue to explore the library in the morning." I thought out loud, "I should be able to absorb a lot more with an awake mind!" My plan seemed flawless, after all the library wasn't going anywhere and for some reason I couldn't take my eyes off the bed.

I slowly walked over to the tunnel to the room. I looked around once more and noticed that the light in this room seemed to be dimming. The books all looked further and further away and before I knew it I was lying down on the bed and fast asleep.

The next morning I woke up and couldn't seem to remember why I decided to sleep in this random bedroom instead of my own. I looked around the small room and could have sworn this room was bigger last night, it seemed like something was missing.

It seemed awfully strange to me. I could only sort of remember a fuzzy dream of running around through winding tunnels and getting lost and found over and over again. The dream was slowly fading by the second and I had already forgotten the last memories of the foggy dream as I headed out of this room and down the stairs.

In the middle of the next night Tristan came back. He sprinted into my room and whispered, "You need to come with me! Hurry and be quiet." We went and woke up Jack. Jack sleepily went and picked up and supported Tom as best as he could. "What is going on?" I asked completely confused by the sudden appearance of the old wizard. "There is no time to explain, we have to head into the basement and hide." The wizard whispered, "And be quiet!" I hobbled as quietly as I could. My leg was particularly stiff in the night's cold.

We headed into the living room. Tristan whispered something and the fireplace opened to reveal a hidden staircase that lead down into the basement.

We went down the staircase as I heard Tristan whisper the spell to close the secret doorway behind us. Right before the doorway shut I heard a high-pitched scream that seemed to be coming from inside my own head. I dropped to my knees in pain, clutching my ears. The scream only lasted for a few seconds and was completely gone by the time the fireplace closed. Everything became extremely frigid during the scream - my breath started fogging up the air. Jack looked like the scream hit him like a punch in the face. He was completely ghost white and he couldn't muster a word. We walked down the hallway past what I assumed were training quarters. Each room we walked by was filled with punching bags, an assortment of weapons, spell books, and armor. We finally reached the end of the hall and went into a cozy room with several chairs surrounding a fireplace. As we all sat down in the chairs, Jack looked as if he still hadn't fully recovered from that ear-piercing scream.

Tristan was the first one to speak, his voice grave, "That scream you all heard back there, that

scream came from one of the Death Raiders."
Tristan looked exhausted as he went on, "There
are only a handful of Death Raiders in
Herobrine's army, but they are some of the most
vicious and foul enemies you'll ever face. They
aren't really even human. They were born in the
same chambers as the creepers, they are
sometimes known as Endermen." A loud crash cut
Tristan off; it came from right above us. "I put as
many protective spells in place before I came
inside, I hope that they can hold this thing off…"
Tristan become quiet, he shot out his arm towards
the fireplace and the logs instantly caught on fire.
Within a few minutes we were all warm again.
Light seemed to return to the world as the
fireplace's shadows danced around the room.

We could all hear the Death Raider trying to break through the protective spells. His repeated smashes were the only thing that we heard for several hours. Finally the constant sound stopped. "Is he gone?" I asked. "We best wait a few more hours just to make sure." Tristan replied. And with that I closed my eyes and went to sleep. I think I could have slept for a whole lifetime and it wouldn't have been enough to make up for these past few days.

I was abruptly woken up. "We need to get out of here now!" Tristan said as he woke me up. "The Death Raiders are coming and we can't be here once they get arrive." Jack jumped to his feet and started picking up Tom. Tristan "I can sense them traveling here as we speak, the first one must have just been a scout."

We headed back up the stairs as fast as we could, through the fireplace, and out the front door. "I brought us horses and weapons!" the old wizard said, "Climb on and let's ride out of here!" I helped Jack with getting Tom on his horse. I then got on my horse as fast as I could. As soon as we were all ready to go we took off! I only just realized that it was snowing out, the forest had transformed into a white winter forest. I wondered if the Death Raiders had caused the cold and the snow. I tried to remember if it was cold on the first night we got here but I couldn't recall.

Our horses were galloping at full speed, and we were blazing our own trail in between the trees. The Death Raiders would be able to track us easily in the snow as each step our horses took left an obvious print in the snow. I knew we either had to outrun the snow or hope for a blizzard to cover our tracks. I was hoping for the first option, as I would rather not travel through a snowstorm.

But it seemed to be growing colder with each passing moment. The falling snow started stinging my face as it came down. The cold wind was biting at my fingers. I pulled my cloak tightly around my neck, hoping for some more warmth. Our horses were slowing down in the cold. I saw the old wizard mutter something under his breath and was instantly greeted by a gush of warm air. "It's not much, but it will do for now" Tristan said. The hot air slowly defrosted my hands; I extended my fingers trying to help heat them up. "Does this cold mean the Death Raiders are on our tail?" I wondered aloud. Tristan replied, "Not necessarily, the Death Raider are practiced in a dark form of magic, their spells are likely to be the true cause of this." Tristan shivered as he spoke, "They must have given up on tracking us and are now hoping to freeze us to death."

The heat spell didn't last much longer. I could feel the last of the warmth drain out of the surroundings. The air was growing colder by the minute. Soon the leaves on trees were completely frozen solid. We rode on for several more hours. I was shivering, trying to stay warm. Finally we broke out of the trees. I could see nothing but snow in all directions. There were no landmarks or any way of figuring out which direction we should head in. Tristan took off without a word. It seemed like it was getting too cold to even speak with one another now.

Our horses slowed down yet again. They couldn't be moving faster than a walking pace now. We just had to hope that we could get out of the radius of this horrible spell before our horses couldn't take it anymore. The amulet sat cold against my chest. Every once in a while Tristan would cast another spell of heat but it would usually only last for a few minutes before it faded back to the utter cold.

I couldn't see any birds or animals; it seemed as if the cold had driven out all the life in this valley. Darkness started covering everything around us as the sun was setting behind the horizon. Night had brought in an even more intense cold. I'm not sure if we could make it much further in this weather. But there was no choice - we had to keep pressing on, we had to try and make it back to the warmth of a city or town.

More hours had passed and we were now riding through the darkest hours of the night. The cold was biting down to the bone. I could barely feel any part of my body. My horse was the last source of heat I had. The heat spells had all but stopped. "LOOK!" Jack yelled, "Is that a trail of smoke!?" He was right. I could just make out a small line of smoke up in the night sky illuminated by the moonlight. Whatever it came from probably had some type of fire! I tried to spur my horse into action, but he didn't seem to believe I had any reason good enough to get him to hurry up. None of the horses seemed to want to ride faster than a slow trot. It was agonizing knowing that there was heat so close but we couldn't get to it any faster.

After what seemed like an eternity the building was finally in view. It was a small inn on the side of a road. The horses finally seemed like they understood why we tried to get them to hurry. They started speeding up anticipating the heat of the inn. We arrived, dismounted, and tied up our horses nearby the small stable fire. They stood as close to the fire as they dared. Jack had to help Tom walk to the Inn. I limped over to the entrance after them. The cold had made my hurt leg entirely stiff. I couldn't even bend it at the knee.

I couldn't believe how warm the Inn felt on my face. My hands were finally thawing out, my body relaxed. The Inn was filled to the brim with people. The sound of music, laughter and singing filled my ears. Everyone who was on that road must have been trying to get out of that cold. We walked over to the innkeeper, she said, "Tristan, I haven't seen you around these parts in a long, long while, what's the occasion?" Tristan smiled and said, "Just thought we would get out of that cold, I don't suppose you have a room for us?" The innkeeper laughed and said "Storms sure are good for business; I hate to say I don't have a single room open!" With the amount of people that were awake and about at this hour of night I wasn't surprised that there was no more room for people to sleep. "You guys can try taking a couple chairs by the fire if you just came from the cold!" The innkeeper said.

I didn't need to be told twice. I headed straight for the closest fireplace and sat down in the nearest chair. The heat slowly seeped through my entire body. From my head to my toes I was completely heated. After I was warmed up I realized how sore I was. I must have clenched all my muscles while we were riding out in the cold, and now I'm paying the price. I'm starting to think we won't get a real break until this war is won, until this is all over. "I am going to sleep for a month when this is over and done with." I said to Jack, who happened to be sitting next to me, he nodded in agreement right before we both passed out.

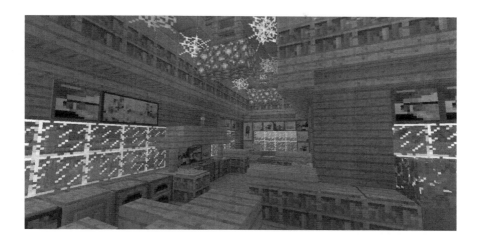

Chapter Four – The Final Stretch

I overheard some of the other people in the Inn talking about the storm, "I was out on the road, doin' my regular delivery run when outta no where comes this blizzard! I didn't even last 30 minutes before I had to come inside here. It's absolutely ridiculous." Everyone listening heartily agreed with him. It seemed like no one else knew why the blizzard came down on us all. I wondered if any one here even knows who the Death Raiders are. Hopefully they don't have to find out.

The heat from the fireplace had warmed me nicely. I fell in and out of sleep for several hours, just relaxing in front of the fire. Finally I noticed that it was light out. It must be morning. I smelled breakfast long before I ever saw it. I only now realized how hungry I was. I didn't remember eating anything in a long time. The Innkeeper brought bacon and mushroom soup around for everyone. I dug in and finished my meal as fast as I could. Tom even woke up enough to be able to drink some soup. It was very quiet during breakfast, everyone had finally fallen asleep hours ago and very few people were even waking up for breakfast.

Tristan was nowhere to be seen. I wondered where he had gone. Hopefully he was still around here somewhere; I decided to ask the innkeeper when she comes around again. "Hey do you know where Tristan went? I haven't seen him in a while." I said, "Oh yeah, he's actually outside taking care of the horses! I'm sure he'll be back inside soon," the innkeeper said reassuringly.

I was thinking about closing my eyes and going back to sleep by this warm fire right as I heard that signature blood curdling scream. It started off really quiet but it quickly grew louder and louder, and soon I could barely stand it. I had to cover my ears to even deal with the pain. The scream finally subsided as Tristan broke through the door and ran over to us. "There isn't much time, you need to listen to me and listen closely Steve." The old wizard spoke quickly, "The amulet around your neck - it's the most important thing we have in this war. You need to use it to destroy the creeper spawners. It's the only way we can destroy them." He looked around as if the Death Raiders were somehow already inside the inn before he went on, "Once the creeper spawners falls this war is won! Do you understand me?!" I nodded my head in response but I couldn't help ask, "Why are you telling me this now?" His face turned grim, "Because you must finish this on your own. I will stay back and hold off the Death Raiders as long as I can. You must go now!"

By now everyone in the inn was scrambling to get away, tables were thrown over, drinks were spilled. It was complete chaos. "Tom, are you able to walk?" I asked, he shook his head yes. I helped him up and reached for the cane. I still needed it to get around with any amount of speed. We all started running towards the door when the roof of the inn was thrown off as the Death Raider arrived. They screamed one more time and caused my friends and me to fall to our knees in agonizing pain. I tried to get my cane up. I pulled my weight back off the ground right as they screamed again. Jack looked as if he was going to pass out during the screams. Finally I was able to get up and keep moving to the door along with my friends.

It had snowed even more throughout the night. Our horses were not happy to see us. They did not want to leave their fire behind and head out into the cold. We finally convinced them that we needed to leave now. Tristan ran outside and began casting a spell. He held out his hand towards the incoming Death Raiders and shouted something in the old language at the top of his lungs. He threw his hands towards them as lightening shot forth and struck the nearest Death Raider head on. The Death raider flew back and didn't get back up. Tristan looked over at us and shouted, "What are you doing just staring! GET A MOVE ON!"

We jumped on our horses and spurred them into action. We looked back at the fading inn right as the wizard cast a massive fireball spell and struck down three Death Raiders with a single blow. We kept on riding as hard as we could. Our horses were pushing through a lot of snow. I looked back one last time to see 4 of the Death Raiders advancing on Tristan. I hope he can get out of there in time. We had to make sure we used this head start that he had given us wisely.

Other people that abandoned the inn were traveling along the road. They were practically going as fast as we were. Some of them were driving their horse drawn carts filled with trading supplies, others were on horseback, and an unlucky few were getting away on foot. We rode our horses fast along the road, with no idea where the road led but all we could do was keep going as fast as we could.

We had been riding for several hours when the snow started to thin out. We must finally be far enough away from the source of the spell. The air seemed warmer and the surrounding area seemed a lot more alive. As we were riding I saw sheep, wolves, and other animals as they walked around.

The further we got away from the inn the warmer and more alive the surroundings seemed. We were still riding close to some of the other people who had escaped from the inn with us. One cart was even keeping pace with us.

After riding for a while we hit our first small town, made up of only about 10 buildings. We decided to take a break from riding, as we were all exhausted. We got off our horses and tacked them up in the towns stable. We hadn't even made it 30 feet before we could feel the air getting colder all around us. "Do you feel that?!" I said to Jack and Tom. "This is not good; we have to get back on our horses!" Jack replied. Tom spoke for the first time in days, "No... They'll spot us on our horses..." His voice trailed off but his eyes lit up as he saw something, "But we could travel in that." He pointed at the horse drawn cart that had traveled along side us from the inn.

"You're a genius!" I said to him. That would give us perfect cover while keeping us moving. We started running over to the cart, looked around, and hopped in the back while no one was watching. This cart looked like it was filled with melons and bags of sugar. It was easy to hide amongst the goods. The cart took off not a second later and started moving down the road with speed.

The air was getting colder and colder. The closer the Death Raiders came the colder the air became. It was starting to get as frigid as it was the other night. Jack peeked out from behind the melons, "I can see them, and it looks like they are right by our horses!" he said, "They must have been able to smell us. Can you see if they are coming this way?" Jack looked up again and replied, "I don't think they know which way we went!" I was relieved, "Hopefully they don't find out! Let's hope that they think we went and hid somewhere in that small town."

We kept our head down and hid for the rest of the day. The cart had traveled non-stop the entire time we had been hiding. The Death Raiders dropped off at some point, the air here was warm, and there was no lingering cold. We had successfully escaped their grasp. I wondered what had happened to Tristan… I'm sure he got away after he gave us the head start.

I peeked out of the back of the cart again and noticed that there were a few houses along the road. We must be headed into town. I looked around and saw that I was the only one awake. Both Tom and Jack were passed out and sleeping on the floor of the moving cart. All of a sudden the road got extremely bumpy. It dawned on me that we must be driving over cobblestone. That could only mean one thing - that we were headed into the city. I peeked over the melons and saw some city streets. The cart must have been on the outskirts of the city. I wondered what city we were in. The bumpy road shook both of my friends awake. They were slowly stretching and yawning as they woke up. "We should probably get off before this cart gets to its destination," I said. The others nodded in agreement.

I climbed over the goods and prepared to jump out, I knew that this was going to hurt my leg… a lot. I braced myself for impact and jumped over the edge. I landed with most of my weight on my good leg but it was still no use. Pain shot up my body as I fell to the ground. I was able to pull myself up with my cane before my friends had jumped out of the back of the cart. "You alright, Steve?" Tom asked, I said, "Yeah, I'll be fine; my leg is still hurt, that's all." We started walking into the heart of the city, "You seem a lot better yourself Tom," I remarked. "Definitely, I feel like I've finally woken up from a month's long coma. That fall was no fun," he responded.

We started heading into the city. It occurred to me that I still didn't know what city this was called. I was thinking about asking someone if they could tell us. I decided it was probably the best idea to figure out where we were. I looked around for someone to ask and all of a sudden realized there was almost no one around. The streets seemed positively empty. "Guys, are you seeing how empty these streets are? There's almost no one around." I quietly said. "That is really creepy, what is going on?" Jack said. I looked behind us and couldn't find a single soul. "Oh no!" Tom sounded panicked. "What is it Tom?" I asked, "Do you know why this city seems so… Abandoned?" Tom looked like he was going to be sick, "This is the abandoned city of Thor…" he seemed like he was going to be sick, "this city was one of the first cities attacked by the Death Raiders at the start of the war, years and years ago, the inhabitants were driven out and the Huntsmen took control of the city. This was back before they even had their creeper army." He looked around, " I had heard rumors that this city was slowly starting to get inhabitants back, but it doesn't really seem like it...I bet that cart driver was just passing through!"

"We can't just stay here in the middle of an empty street; we should get inside one of these buildings!" I said. Everyone agreed and we all ran to the nearest house. We were now much closer to the center of the city. Jack kicked in the door and we all ran inside. We had just entered an abandoned inn. I lit up the closest torch to brighten up the dark, dark room. We all sat down at the nearest table. It was extremely eerie. The whole place seemed like a ghost town.

"Well, what are we going to do now?" Jack asked, exasperated. Tom looked up, "I think I might actually know what we could do here," he went on with his plan, "I was just thinking about how nobody knows where the creeper spawners actually are. It could be anywhere for all we know. But they would probably put it somewhere close to their capital, but also close to the front lines. They also wouldn't build their spawners near a lot of people. I think it's possible that they build the creeper spawners right here, under the city of Thor."

I said, "That does make a lot of sense, but we would still need to figure out how to get to the creeper spawners." Tom nodded in agreement, "I think I know how we can find the entrance and how we can get in. We have to use your amulet!"

I was surprised to hear that Tom knew anything about my amulet, let alone what it was capable of, "How do you know all this?" I asked. Tom smiled, "I dreamed about it, Steve." "Ha ha very funny Tom, how do you really know?" Jack said sarcastically. "I'm not kidding. I had a lot of dreams while I was out. Tristan visited me in several of them and explained everything he knew about the amulet." I didn't doubt him, I still remember seeing my brother in my dreams and thinking it was nothing more than a dream. It turned out to be more real than I ever imagined.

Tom went on, "The amulet should be pointing to the entrance after you spin it. As long as you are near the entrance when you spin it around, it will point you straight to the door." "That was easier than I was expecting" Jack said. I agreed, "Well let's get started then!"

We decided to try the first spin right there in the inn. I pulled the amulet off from around my neck and put it down in the center of the table. "Let me just spin it," I said as I reached over and flicked the amulet around. The amulet instantly came to life; it twirled around and around for ages until it finally settled on some direction pointing to the right. "Wow I can't believe that actually worked!"

I exclaimed, "Let's get going and find that entrance!"

We didn't skip another beat, and headed straight outside. I looked down at the amulet and spun it in my hand. The constant rotation warmed up my hand. Finally it stopped spinning; the amulet looked like it was pointing towards the city center. "Into the city center we go" I remarked. We headed further into the city, but it still seemed far too creepy and weird to see such an abandoned city, with no people going to the shops, walking around, or even just heading home. It was completely empty. That cart driver from earlier was nowhere to be seen. As we advanced into the city center, the shops and buildings started to get more compacted and the buildings became taller.

Finally we walked into a square with 5 streets coming off it. I let the amulet spin slowly in my hand. "It's spinning around - I don't know what it's doing," I said. Tom came over and looked at the amulet, "I think we might be over top of the entrance! It must be located somewhere down in the sewers below." I looked around and wasn't sure if I could see an entrance to the sewers anywhere. "Over there," Jack said, "I can see a 'sewer access' sign on that building!"

We all ran over to the door, but it was locked. It didn't take another second for Jack to use his signature kick to break it down. This was the right place all right. I instantly smelled the sewers, and it was awful. I went in first and started climbing the ladder down into the pipes. With every rung of the ladder the smell got worse. At the bottom I could hardly stand to breathe because the smell was so bad. "Wow that is awful. What do you guys say we just head home now?" Jack joked.

The amulet started going haywire again; it was spinning back and forth without pointing in any real direction any more. I kept on walking the way it was originally pointing hoping that I could get a good reading again soon. As I walked further and further down the tunnel the spinning only got worse. We had come up to a dead end without any obvious path forward. "What does the amulet say now?" Tom asked. "I don't know it's spinning around again…" I muttered, slightly disappointed, "Maybe we need to go further down."

Jack was the first of us to spot the sewer grate under our feet; it was almost perfectly disguised as the stone floor all around us. "Here help me lift this out of the way." Jack said as he bent down and grabbed ahold of the grate. Marvin and I moved into position and pulled as hard as we could. Slowly inch-by-inch the grate lifted out of place and came free. "Whoa, would you look at that!" Jack said in amazement. Underneath the grate was a beautiful stone staircase heading down further into the ground. It seemed ancient and protected, as if it hadn't been disturbed in years and years.

Marvin adjusted his footing right as he lost his balance and slipped straight down the stairs, hitting every single step on the way down. "Are you alright down there?" I yelled. "Yeah I should be fine, I'm just a bit more bruised now is all," Marvin called back with a bit of pain in his voice. "Let's go after him," I said as I motioned to Jack.

The stairs were a lot longer than I had imagined, Tom must have really had a bad time going down all of this. Jack was right behind me keeping pace. All the while the amulet kept spinning around and around never picking a direction. "Guys, I think this amulet isn't going to work…" I said, my voice echoed off the walls, "It was working fine for a while but it hasn't stopped spinning in ages."

Right as I got to the bottom of the stairs the amulet snapped to attention, it was pointing straight ahead and almost vibrating with excitement. "Hang on! I think it's working again!" I said enthusiastically. I started walking forward; Tom had already helped himself to his feet and didn't look too damaged. He gave a sheepish smile as he started walking. All along this hallway were smaller hallways to the left and right; each one seemed to go on for ages. As I passed the first walkway the amulet snapped and pointed straight at it. As soon as I moved forward the amulet shot around and pointed at the next hallway. It did this as we passed every hallway, never deciding which one it wanted to go in.

I noticed one of the hallways had a light on, the light spilled onto the walls al around it. "There! Let's see if this is the right hallway!" I said as we moved towards it. The amulet stopped snap back and forth and instead began spinning around again. It got worse and worse, as we got closer to the lit up hallway. A figure darted out of the hallway and faced us, "WHO GOES HERE! WHY DO YOU WIELD THE AMULET!?" the voice screamed at us with vicious intent.

"Wha-, who are you?!" I stumbled back at him. The figure came into view, it was an old man, he couldn't have been more than a few years away from dying, he seemed so frail and yet there was an energy about him. "WHY. DO. YOU. HAVE. THE. AMULET!" he screamed back in reply.

"It's mine," I defended, "I'm using it to find the secret entrance in the sewer system." The old man looked at the three of us and realized we were only 3 harmless young boys. "Well, well, well, would you look at that. I never thought anyone would come." The old man said, his voice had softened, "You are trying to rid this world of the Huntsmen, no?" We nodded our heads in response. "Well that explains how you go here, I've spent years down here waiting for the amulet, hoping I didn't need to pry it from the Huntsmen's hands. I'm one of the last inhabitants of this city, I never could leave it behind, so I decided I would be useful and help in whatever small way I could."

The old man continued," I cast a spell on this place ensuring who ever had the amulet would be lured into my trap. Admittedly the trap didn't go off but that's probably for the best!" The old man all of a sudden seemed tired and wary. "I suppose I can't hold you here forever, the Huntsmen need to be stopped and soon. I will lift the spell, just start walking that way and I will make sure that amulet functions right! GOODBYE!" and just like that the old man disappeared back into your hallway, the light that lit it went out not two seconds later. I looked over at Tom and Jack and they both looked just as surprised and stunned as I did.

My amulet slowly calmed down in my hand. Finally it was pointing in the direction of a random hallway about 40 blocks down. We went down this walkway and continued in a straight line for what seemed like an eternity.
I looked back down at my amulet and followed it down one of the sewer pipes. After a few minutes of walking I noticed the flickering shadows of a torch around a corner. It hadn't occurred to me that the entrance would be guarded. I whispered, "We're going to need to be as quiet as we can. We might be able to sneak by whatever is up ahead."

I crouched ahead, and walked as quietly as I could. I slowly came up to the bend in the pipe and peered around the corner. I saw a staircase heading further down into the ground. Guarding it was one of the Huntsmen sleeping in a chair in front of the entrance. "Perfect! He's asleep. We can slip right by," I whispered back to my friends.

Walking as quietly as I could, I inched closer to the staircase, Jack and Tom just behind me. I was almost there… Just a few more feet and I'd sneak right by him. I didn't even realize that my amulet was starting to slip out of my hand; before I could do anything it started falling to the floor! In a flash Jack had just caught the amulet only a couple of inches above the floor. I looked over the guard he hadn't noticed a thing. I sheepishly smiled back at Jack as he handed back the amulet.

I kept moving towards the entrance and finally slipped by the guard, my friends following right behind me.

I started going down the staircase. I heard the sounds of the creeper spawners. New creepers were making their signature noises. It terrified me to the bone. I really hoped that this would work. The amulet was my only hope of making it through all of this. I kept going down the staircase. After a few minutes of walking we reached a fork in the path. It was eerily similar to the great mountain and their inner chambers. The only difference is that these hallways were absolutely massive; I could barely see the ceiling.

Before I knew what was happening a heard a yell out in the distance, "Who goes there!" I heard the sounds of marching feet approaching. We all tried to hide as best as we could, but it was no use. I knew we were going to be captured. I decided to save my friends and sacrifice myself. It was the least I could do for them coming with me all this way and sticking by my side. They saw me through this whole thing, they had stood by me and now I was going to stick by them. I whispered, "Whatever you see, stay hidden, you can still destroy the creeper spawners..." I handed Tom the amulet and stepped out into the open.

"You were looking for me?" I said tauntingly holding out my hands. I started sprinting in the opposite direction trying to lead them away from my friends and from the amulet. I looked back as I was running and saw that the guards were hot on my heels. It would only be a few more seconds until they caught up to me. One of the Huntsmen jumped out and took me down. I looked back and saw exactly what I had feared, my friends had been caught too, and there were simply too many soldiers for them to be able to hide.

I hung my head down as the soldiers took us away; we had failed in our mission. The creeper spawners were still active, pumping out a new creeper army for the Huntsmen. I failed the Greenskeepers. I looked at my friends and they both had the same look in their eye. They knew we had been defeated. Our plan had failed.

They were taking us away to their jail cells. Similar to the ones my brother was kept in at the Great Mountain. I could finally see the cells in the distance. There were other Greenskeeper prisoners, soldiers that had been sneaking through the city of Thor, and others were probably caught in the same way we were.

Right as we were approaching the cells I heard a familiar voice in the distance. "LEAVE THEM ALONE" Tristan's voice boomed through out the hallways, a flash of light exploded out from his hands, knocking all the guards down around us.

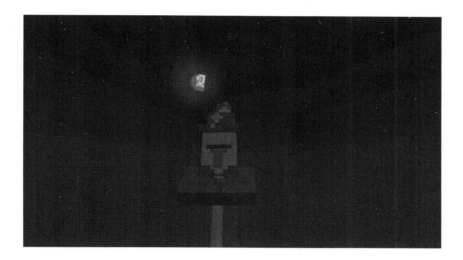

We didn't hesitate for another second. All of us started running towards Tristan, "Let's hurry down to the core of the spawners before the entire army arrives!" I shouted as I ran past Tristan. This would be our last chance to destroy them. Jack threw the amulet to me as I ran past.

I had never run so fast in my life. My friends were right behind me as I ran, but I could hear the Huntsmen right behind us. The old wizard set off a few spells to give us more time. Finally we made it down the hallway and into the great chambers where the spawners were housed. I saw the very core, the little black cage that spawns each and every creeper. There were hundreds of creepers in this room. As soon as they saw us, they began running towards us in one uniform mass of destruction.

I felt the amulet heat up in my hand as I got closer and closer to the spawner. I would need to get through this crowd of creepers if I wanted to get close enough to destroy the spawners. "Tristan, I could really use some help clearing a path!" I shouted. "I'm already on it," Tristan replied. His spell ripped through the crowd of creepers with a single blow. I saw my opportunity and took it. I ran straight through the middle of the crowd in the opening that the wizard had created. I heard some creepers explode behind me. I ran harder and harder, the amulet was hot to the touch now. The creepers started closing in on me, but I had almost broken through the crowd.

Just as the creepers closed in I sprinted and jumped, sliding across the floor and out of the creeper horde. The creeper spawner was now in range. I aimed the amulet as I ran and before I knew it, its blinding light had filled the great room. A thunderous crash emitted from the amulet.

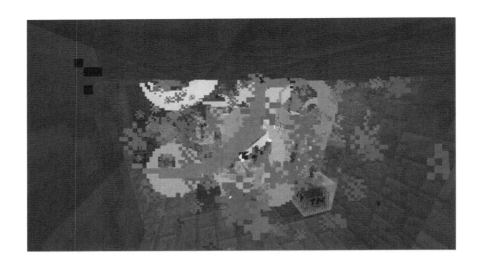

I passed out right after I felt a huge shockwave rip through the creeper crowd, destroying them all…

"…Place that block right over here! That's perfect!" I remarked. The maze is basically complete now! I hobbled over to the entrance of our newly built maze. "Wow, this thing has really came together!" Jack said. It had been several weeks since we won the war. After the creeper spawners were destroyed it was a simple swoop in to end what little was left of the Huntsmen. Herobrine fled off into the mountains, his army destroyed. We had one the war. My brother was one of the final attackers on the enemy capital. He should be back any day now!

My adventure had left me with a newfound appreciation for life and for adventure. I was still a builder first but I wouldn't say no to a little trip out into the unknown from now on.

Bonus section

Thank you for reading this book. I hope you enjoyed it. Gaming is very near and dear to my heart and I enjoy every moment I spend playing my favourite games.

If you liked this book, and are interested in more, I invite you to join my "Customer Only" newsletter at http://awesomeguides.net/. I publish all my best stuff there for free, only for my customers.

If you're a Minecraft fan like I am, I'm sure you'll like my other best-selling releases:

1. Minecraft: Awesome Building Ideas for You
2. Amazing Minecraft Secrets You Never Knew About
3. Minecraft All-In-One Quick Guide! Master your Minecraft skills in Everything!

4. The Amazing Tale of Steve: A Minecraft Novel
5. Minecraft: Amazing House Designs with step-by-step instruction
6. Awesome Minecraft Traps To Defend Your Home
7. 50 Awesome Minecraft Seeds That You NEED to Know
8. Amazing Minecraft Maps You Will Definitely Enjoy!
9. Minecraft Amazing Redstone Contraptions
10. The Ultimate Minecraft Guide to Tekkit: Discover the Advanced Mods for Minecraft!

In my strategy guides, I share neat tips and tricks to help you get better at gaming. From Candy Crush to Dragonvale, you'll find strategy guides for a wide variety of addictive games.

1. The Last of Us: Amazing Strategies and Secrets

2. <u>Dragonvale: The Complete Guide: Amazing Cheats, Gems, Breeding and MORE!</u>
3. <u>Candy Crush Saga Best Tips, Tricks and Cheats!</u>

We also have an awesome Minecraft course on Udemy – an instructor led online learning platform.

1. <u>All about Minecraft: A complete educational course</u>

Have fun gaming!
Egor

Made in the USA
San Bernardino, CA
06 July 2014